His Holiness the Dalai Lama

His Holiness
the Dalai Lama

In My Own Words

Compiled and edited by
MARY CRAIG

Hodder & Stoughton
LONDON   SYDNEY   AUCKLAND

British Library Cataloguing in Publication Data
A record for this book is available from the British Library

ISBN 0 340 785357

Typeset in Adobe Goudy Old Style by
Strathmore Publishing Services, London N7

Printed and bound in Great Britain by
Clays Ltd, St Ives PLC

Hodder and Stoughton
A Division of Hodder Headline Ltd
338 Euston Road
London NW1 3BH

CONTENTS

INTRODUCTION

In the late 1980s, when I first became dimly aware of
the plight of Tibet, it was actually the prospect of an
audience with His Holiness the Fourteenth Dalai Lama
which sent me off to his place of exile in Dharamsala,
North India, to investigate the possibilities of a book.
Tibet was a virtually unknown quantity as far as I was
concerned, but the chance of an audience was too
good to miss. Though I expected little more than
an exchange of platitudes, I was curious to meet this
exotic figure who, in my limited imagination, would
come straight out of Shangri La by way of Lost Horizon.

Little did I realise that this visit would turn me up-
side down and inside out. I returned home filled with
fury, pity and disgust for the sufferings of the Tibetans
at the hands of their Chinese conquerors – and deter-
mined to tell the world what had been done to them.
As for the Dalai Lama, within minutes of meeting him,
I found myself reflecting that here was the most human

human being I had ever met. Along with a luminous simplicity and warmth he radiated serenity and a deep inner peace. He had that rare gift of speaking directly to the human heart and evoking a response. In their different ways, this and all my subsequent encounters with him were life-enhancing.

After he won the Nobel Peace Prize in 1989, he became better known and began to criss-cross the globe with his message of peace and love. Millions of people became aware of him and in the West he gained a huge and growing following. Ask anyone today to list the names of those who have left a spiritual imprint on our materialistic times, and the Dalai Lama will be up there alongside Gandhi, Mother Teresa, Martin Luther King and Good Pope John. His is one of the truly prophetic voices of our time. He is one of those rare beings capable of reaching out to a Western society that, for all its prosperity and high degree of material comfort, is bewildered and confused, and needs all the help it can get.

There is an irony in all this. The Dalai Lama carries his message of peace and hope to the Western world, simply because, since 1959, he has been in exile from his own country and his Buddhist teachings are proscribed by the Chinese Communists who have ruled Tibet mercilessly since they invaded it fifty years ago.

It is perhaps because he knows the anguish of his people and has himself suffered the pains of loss and alienation that he is able to empathise so profoundly with the spiritual angst and emptiness that he perceives all around him.

His message is a simple one, some would say simplistic: material prosperity alone is not capable of satisfying us. True happiness cannot lie in the mere gratification of our sensual desires – for in the long run, the senses are incapable of ever being appeased. The happiness of any society depends on the inner contentment of those who compose it, yet in our modern societies such peace of mind is sadly lacking. Only an inner discipline can bring us to calmness of mind via the conviction that humanity cannot survive except through kindness, love and compassion. Over and over again he asserts his belief that in spite of evidence to the contrary, human nature is basically good, gentle and unaggressive. Compassion lies at the heart of what we are; we are social creatures, dependent on each other, and the aim of life should be to eradicate the negative thoughts and emotions that beset us and develop what he calls 'the good heart' – which acts out of a desire to help others. Compassion for each other's pain and suffering alone makes us human. 'That we humans can help each other is one of our unique

human capacities,' he says. The development of
compassion allied with wisdom is and must necessarily
be at the heart of all religions, uniting them as nothing
else could. And so he calls for nothing less than a
spiritual revolution, a radical transformation which
will take us away from our seemingly endemic preoccupation with ourselves and force us into a heartfelt
concern for the happiness of the whole human family
and, by extension, a sense of responsibility for all
sentient beings and for the entire planet.

As we enter the new millennium and the twenty-
first century, he warns against too facile a belief that
a new century will of itself sweep away the world's ills.
'That is wrong,' he says. 'Unless there is a new millennium inside, then the new millennium will not change
much – same days and nights, same sun and moon.
The important thing is transformation, new ways of
thinking.' He dreams of a world in which truth and
justice will prevail and peace can become a reality. A
demilitarised, democratic world in which human rights
are respected: 'There can be no peace as long as there
is grinding poverty, social injustice, inequality, oppression, environmental degradation, and as long as the
weak and small continue to be down-trodden by the
mighty and powerful.' A pipe-dream perhaps, but he
is convinced that such a world will never come about

through violent means, for 'violence ultimately leads to the betrayal of even the noblest cause.' His belief in the Gandhian ideal of non-violence as a way to solve the problems of the world may seem naïve to some but is crucial to him. It leads to another equally difficult belief, forgiveness of the enemy, a Christian belief too, though more honoured in the breach than the observance. For me, nothing is more moving or powerful than the Dalai Lama's steadfast and humbling refusal to hate those who have hated and persecuted him and his people. He would go further: it is only by learning to forgive those who do harm to us that we can learn the difficult virtues of patience and tolerance, and thus learn to master ourselves. As I write this, the Dalai Lama has been visiting Belfast, to try to inject a note of sanity into that sadly hate-torn province. In Derry, where he met Catholic and Protestant victims of violence, there was at first an air of suspicion. But the tension lifted when a woman came to thank him for relieving her of a burden she had carried for ten years – of being unable to forgive the men who'd murdered her husband. She had always felt that to forgive would be to betray his memory. But listening that day to the words of the Dalai Lama, she had become convinced that the only way to find healing lay in trying to forgive.

A great spiritual teacher then. Yet, in August 2000, following pressure from the Chinese, the Dalai Lama was not invited to the Spiritual Leaders' Summit organised in New York by the United Nations. And when his New York representative read out a message from him, Chinese religious leaders walked out in protest. It was not the first time that a snub of this kind had been administered. In 1995 he was excluded from the UN's Fiftieth Anniversary celebrations, and from an interfaith service in New York. (Speakers at anniversary functions have to be officially approved, and China is a key member of the Security Council, with power of veto.) The UN was also accused of censorship for expunging a quotation on Human Rights from its commemorative book, *A Vision of Hope*. The offending quotation read: 'It is in the inherent nature of human beings to yearn for freedom, equality and dignity and they have an equal right to achieve that … Brute force, no matter how strongly applied, can never subdue the basic desire for freedom and dignity.' In respect of his fellow Tibetans, however, that basic yearning has been consistently ignored by the world at large.

Cynics say that, sincere though he undoubtedly is, he repeats himself, saying the same thing over and over again in his lectures, addresses, teachings, question-and-answer sessions, never venturing into originality. But when the health and harmony of the human race are at stake, does that really matter? The message really is simple, and maybe it is only by constant repetition that it will eventually be absorbed. There is always a danger that the thousands who flock to hear the Dalai Lama are mesmerised by the charisma of the man himself but do not really listen to what he is telling them, still less put it into practice.

That he exerts an undeniable power for good was well illustrated by a *New York Times* journalist, A. M. Rosenthal, when the Dalai Lama's visit to the USA in 1999 coincided with an upsurge in street violence. Rosenthal faced a dilemma. Should his weekly column deal with the street shooting in LA or the message of the Dalai Lama? 'I did not want to write about the shootings ... and would not,' he finally decided. 'The reason is that I had planned to write about the power, in a man I know, of human goodness. If I wrote this column about a killer, his evil would, for this day in this space, conquer my friend and his value to the world – and I could not permit that to happen.'

I have chosen the excerpts in this anthology with that in mind – to bring the power of human goodness exemplified by Tenzin Gyatso, the Fourteenth Dalai Lama, to readers who may, in part, be unfamiliar with his teachings. I have chosen those which are simple, accessible and capable of bringing much-needed hope to a confused and confusing world.

MARY CRAIG

Looking for Happiness in a Secular Society

*I am a simple Buddhist monk,
no more, no less.*

Compassion for others (as opposed to self) is one of the central teachings of Mahayana Buddhism. In this connection I would like to quote a verse which conveys the message:

> If you are unable to exchange your happiness
> For the suffering of other beings,
> You have no hope of attaining Buddhahood,
> Or even of happiness in this present life.

ADDRESS, 1963

I come from the East, most of you [here] are Westerners. If I look at you superficially, we are different, and if I put my emphasis on that level, we grow more distant. If I look on you as my own kind, as human beings like myself, with one nose, two eyes, and so forth, then automatically that distance is gone. We are the same human flesh. I want happiness; you also want happiness. From that mutual recognition, we can build respect and real trust for each other. From that can come co-operation and harmony.

3

*F*or my own part, meeting innumerable people from all over the world and from every walk of life reminds me of our basic sameness as human beings. Indeed, the more I see of the world, the clearer it becomes that, no matter what our situation, whether we are rich or poor, educated or not, of one race, gender, religion or another, we all desire to be happy and to avoid suffering. Our every intended action, in a sense our whole life – how we choose to live it within the context of the limitations imposed by our circumstances – can be seen as our answer to the great question which confronts us all – 'How am I to be happy?'

*M*aterial progress alone is not sufficient to achieve an ideal society. Even in countries where great external progress has been made mental problems have increased, causing additional hardships. No amount of legislation or coercion can accomplish the well-being of society, for this depends upon the internal attitude of the people who compose it.

ADDRESS, 1981

*G*enerally speaking, even if money brings us happiness, it tends to be the kind which money can buy: material things and sensory experiences. And these, we discover, become a source of suffering themselves. As far as actual possessions are concerned, we must admit that they often cause us more not less difficulty in life. The car breaks down, we lose our money, our most precious belongings are stolen, our house is damaged by fire. Or we worry about these things happening.

*T*he problem is not materialism as such. Rather it is the underlying assumption that full satisfaction can arise from gratifying the senses alone. Unlike animals whose quest for happiness is restricted to survival and to the immediate gratification of sensory desires, we human beings have the capacity to experience happiness at a deeper level which, when achieved, can overwhelm unhappy experiences.

*I*ndeed, if we compare the rich with those who are poor, it often seems that those with nothing are in fact those with the least anxiety, though they may be plagued with physical pains and suffering. As for the rich, whilst a few know how to use their wealth intelligently – that is to say not in luxurious living but sharing it with the needy – most do not. Many are so caught up with the idea of acquiring still more that they make no room for anything else in their lives. In their absorption they actually lose the dream of happiness which riches were to have provided. As a result, they are constantly torn between doubt about what might happen and the hope of gaining more. They are plagued with mental and emotional suffering – even though they may outwardly appear to be leading entirely successful and comfortable lives. This is evident in the disturbing prevalence of anxiety, discontent, frustration, uncertainty, doubt and depression among the populations of the materially developed countries. To my mind, such inner suffering clearly reflects a growing confusion in respect of what morality consists in and what its foundations are.

The brief elation we experience appeasing sensual impulses is very close to what the drug addict feels when indulging his or her habit. Temporary relief is soon followed by a craving for more. And in just the same way that taking drugs in the end only causes trouble, so too does much of what we undertake to fulfil our immediate sensory desires. This is not to say that the pleasure we take in certain activities is somehow mistaken. But we must acknowledge that there can be no hope of gratifying the senses permanently. At best, the happiness we derive from eating a good meal can only last until the next time we are hungry.

Real love is not based on attachment, but on altruism. In this case, your compassion will remain as a humane response to suffering as long as beings continue to suffer.

We humans are social beings. We come into the world as the result of others' actions. We survive here in dependence on others. Whether we like it or not, there is hardly a moment of our lives in which we do not benefit from others' activities. For this reason it is hardly surprising that most of our happiness arises in the context of our relationships with others. Nor is it so remarkable that our greatest joy should come when we are motivated by concern for others. But that is not all. We find that not only do altruistic actions bring about happiness, but they also lessen our experience of suffering. Here I am not suggesting that the individual whose actions are motivated by the wish to bring others happiness necessarily meets with less misfortune than the one who does not. Sickness, old age, mishaps of one sort or another are the same for us all. But the sufferings which undermine our internal peace – anxiety, doubt, disappointment – these are definitely less.

*A*s long as there is a lack of the inner discipline that brings calmness of mind, no matter what external facilities or conditions you have, they will never give you the feeling of joy and happiness that you are seeking. On the other hand, if you possess this inner quality of calmness of mind, a degree of stability within, then even if you lack various external facilities that you would normally consider necessary for happiness, it is still possible to live a happy and joyful life.

*T*he basic fact is that humanity survives through kindness, love and compassion. That human beings can develop these qualities is their real blessing.

*N*o matter how wealthy we are, we have only ten fingers on which to display our rings.

TALK AT SMITHSONIAN FOLKLIFE FESTIVAL,
WASHINGTON DC, JULY 2000

Compassion can be roughly defined in terms of a state of mind that is non-violent, non-harming and non-aggressive. It is a mental attitude based on the wish for others to be free of their sufferings and is associated with a sense of commitment, responsibility and respect towards others …

In one sense, one could define compassion as the feeling of unbearableness at the sight of other people's suffering. And in order to generate that feeling one must first have an appreciation of the seriousness or intensity of another's suffering. So I think that the more fully one understands suffering and the various kinds of suffering that we are subject to, the deeper will be our level of compassion.

One of my fundamental convictions is that basic human nature is more disposed toward compassion and affection. Basic human nature is gentle, not aggressive or violent ... I would also argue that when we examine the relationship between mind – or consciousness – and body, we see that wholesome attitudes, emotions, and states of mind, like compassion, tolerance and forgiveness, are strongly connected with physical health and well-being. They enhance physical well-being, whereas negative or unwholesome attitudes and emotions – anger, hatred, disturbed states of mind – undermine physical health.

We have to build inner strength to develop our self-confidence. Compassion actually brings us more inner strength, more self-confidence so we can more easily communicate with our fellow human beings.

NEWS CONFERENCE DURING USA VISIT,
AUGUST 1999

*T*he purpose of life is the development of a good warm heart … With this quality, you will lead your whole life meaningfully.

*W*ithout love we could not survive. Human beings are social creatures, and a concern for each other is the very basis of our life together.

THE
REAL
TROUBLEMAKERS

*As human beings we have good qualities
as well as bad ones. Now, anger, attachment,
jealousy, hatred, are the bad side; these are the
real enemy ... The true troublemaker is inside.*

ADDRESS, 1994

*I*n Buddhism, any thought, feeling or mental state that undermines our peace of mind from within – all negative thoughts and emotions such as anger, pride, lust, greed, envy and so on, are considered to be afflictions.

We tend to imagine these negative thoughts and emotions to be an integral part of our mind about which we can do very little. Far from recognising their destructive potential and challenging them, we often nurture and reinforce them. But ... their nature is wholly destructive. They are the very source of un-ethical conduct. They are also the basis of the worry, depression, confusion and stress which are such a feature of modern society.

*A*nger is the real destroyer of our good human qualities; an enemy with a weapon cannot destroy these qualities, but anger can. Anger is our real enemy.

*I*f we live our lives continually motivated by anger and hatred, even our physical health deteriorates.

*A*nger or hatred is like a fisherman's hook. It is very important for us to ensure that we are not caught by it.

*W*e have a saying in Tibet: 'If you lose your temper and get angry, bite your knuckles.' This means that if you lose your temper, do not show it to others. Rather, say to yourself, 'Leave it'.

*A*t a time when people are so conscious of maintaining their physical health by controlling their diets, exercising and so forth, it makes sense to try to cultivate the corresponding positive mental attitudes too.

ADDRESS, 1963

*A*ccording to Buddhist psychology, most of our troubles are due to our passionate desire for, attachment to things that we misapprehend as enduring entities. The pursuit of the objects of our desire and attachment involves the use of aggression and competitiveness … These mental processes easily translate into actions, breeding belligerence. Such processes have been going on in the human mind since time immemorial, but their execution has become more effective under modern conditions. What can we do to control and regulate these 'poisons' – delusion, greed and aggression? For it is these poisons that are behind almost every trouble in the world.

*H*atred can be the greatest stumbling block to the development of compassion and happiness. If you can learn to develop patience and tolerance towards your enemies, then everything becomes much easier – your compassion towards all others begins to flow naturally.

*H*appiness cannot come from hatred or anger. Nobody can say, 'Today I am happy because this morning I was very angry.' On the contrary, people feel uneasy and sad and say, 'Today I am not very happy, because I lost my temper this morning.' Through kindness, whether at our own level or at the national and international level, through mutual understanding and through mutual respect, we will get peace, we will get happiness, and we will get genuine satisfaction.

ADDRESS, 1963

*T*he true antidote to greed is contentment. If you have a strong sense of contentment, it doesn't matter whether you obtain the object of your desire or not. Either way, you are still content.

RELIGION, RELIGIONS AND NO RELIGION AT ALL

I am not promoting Buddhism.
I am promoting human values.

ADDRESS TO A BUDDHIST TEACHERS'
CONFERENCE IN CALIFORNIA,
JULY 2000

I am not interested in converting other people to Buddhism, but in how we Buddhists can contribute to human society, according to our own ideas. I believe that other religious faiths also think in a similar way, seeking to contribute to the common aim.

Because the different religions have at times argued with each other rather than concentrating on how to contribute to a common aim, for the last twenty years, in India, I have taken every opportunity to meet with Christian monks – Catholic and Protestant – as well as Muslims, Jews, and, of course, many Hindus. We meet, pray together, meditate together, and discuss their philosophical ideas, their approach, their techniques. I take great interest in Christian practices, in what we can learn and copy from their system. Similarly, in Buddhist theory there may be points such as meditative techniques which can be practised in the Christian church.

I think it is quite possible that a person who is basically a Christian, who accepts the idea of a God, who believes in God, could at the same time incorporate certain Buddhist ideas and techniques into his/her practice. The teachings of love, compassion and kindness are present in Christianity and also in Buddhism ... While remaining committed to Christianity it is quite conceivable that a person may choose to undergo training in meditation, concentration, and one-pointedness of mind, that, while remaining a Christian, one may choose to practise Buddhist ideas.

*R*eligion should never become a source of conflict, a further factor of division within the human community. For my own part ... I continue to take teachings from as many different traditions as possible.

I see all the different religious traditions as paths for the development of inner peace, which is the true foundation of world peace. These ancient traditions come to us as a gift from our common past. Will we continue to cherish it as a gift and hand it over to the future generations as a legacy of our shared desire for peace? Or will we turn it into another weapon that will snatch away the future of the coming generations? The choice we will make is obvious. What needs detailed discussion is how we can ensure that the different religions of the world can become powerful allies of peace.

AUGUST 2000 – THE DALAI LAMA'S MESSAGE
TO THE UN MILLENNIUM WORLD PEACE SUMMIT,
TO WHICH, OWING TO PRESSURE FROM CHINA,
HE HAD NOT BEEN INVITED

*W*hat we call Buddha is warm-heartedness developed infinitely, love perfected. Also infinite enlightened consciousness.

ADDRESS AT WESTMINSTER ABBEY,
LONDON, 1985

*T*he world's religions can contribute to world peace
if there is peace and growing harmony between the different
faiths. It would be tragic if inter-religious rivalry
and conflict undermines world peace in the twenty-first
century. In this regard, I have always encouraged
and supported efforts towards better understanding
among our different faiths. It is my firm belief that this
better understanding will enhance the ability of different
faiths to make positive contributions to world
peace … Religious and spiritual leaders can play a
pivotal role by making a sustained effort to explain to
their respective followers the importance of respecting
the beliefs and tradition of other faiths. We need to
embrace the spirit of pluralism in religion also.

ADDRESS AT WESTMINSTER ABBEY,
LONDON, 1985

*T*he greater our awareness is regarding the value and effectiveness of other religious traditions, then the deeper will be our respect and reverence towards other religions. This is the proper way for us to promote genuine compassion and a spirit of harmony among the religions of the world.

I would like to mention my visit to Lourdes as a pilgrim. There, in front of the cave, I experienced something very special. I felt a spiritual vibration, a kind of spiritual presence there. And then, in front of the image of the Virgin Mary, I prayed. I expressed my admiration for this holy place that has long been a source of inspiration and strength, that has provided spiritual solace, comfort and healing to millions of people. And I prayed that this may continue for a long time to come. My prayer there was not directed to any clearly defined object, like Buddha or Jesus Christ or a bodhisattva, but was simply directed to all great beings who have infinite compassion towards all sentient beings.

*I*f we view the world's religions from the widest possible viewpoint, and examine their ultimate goals, we find that [they all] are directed to the achievement of permanent human happiness ... All religions emphasise the fact that the true follower must be honest and gentle, in other words, that a truly religious person must always strive to be a better human being. To this end, the different religions teach different doctrines which will help transform the person. In this regard, all religions are the same, there is no conflict ...

Now from the philosophical point of view, the theory that God is the creator, is almighty and permanent, is in contradiction to the Buddhist teachings. From this point of view there is disagreement. For Buddhists, the universe has no first cause and hence no creator, nor can there be any such thing as a permanent, primordially pure being. So, of course, doctrinally there is conflict. The views are opposite to one another. But if we consider the *purpose* of these different philosophies, then we see that they are the same.

*T*he purpose of religion is not to build beautiful churches or temples, but to cultivate positive human qualities such as tolerance, generosity and love. Every world religion, no matter what its philosophical view, is founded first and foremost on the precept that we must reduce our selfishness and serve others. Unfortunately, sometimes, in the name of religion, people cause more quarrels than they solve. Practitioners of different faiths should realise that each religious tradition has immense intrinsic value as a means for providing mental and spiritual health.

ADDRESS TO THE PARLIAMENTARY EARTH SUMMIT OF THE UN CONFERENCE ON ENVIRONMENT AND DEVELOPMENT, RIO DE JANEIRO, JUNE 1992

The development of love and compassion is basic and I usually say that this is the main message of religion. When we speak of religion we need not refer to deeper philosophical issues ... The important thing is that in your daily life you practise the essential things, and on that level there is hardly any difference between Buddhism, Christianity, or any other religion. All religions emphasise betterment, improving human beings, a sense of brotherhood and sisterhood, love.

Tibet was a Buddhist nation for many centuries. Naturally that resulted in Tibetans feeling that Buddhism was the best religion, and a tendency to feel that it would be a good thing if all of humanity became Buddhist ... And that kind of extreme thinking just causes problems. But now that we've left Tibet, we've had a chance to come into contact with other religious traditions and learn about them. This has resulted in [our] coming closer to reality, realising that among human beings there are so many different mental dispositions. Even if we tried to make the whole world Buddhist it would be impracticable.

*W*hen we compare two ancient spiritual traditions like Buddhism and Christianity, what we see is a striking similarity between the narratives of the founding masters: in the case of Christianity, Jesus Christ, and in the case of Buddhism, the Buddha. I see a very important parallel: in the very lives of the [founders] the essence of their teachings is demonstrated. For example ... the essence of the Buddha's teaching is embodied in the Four Noble Truths: the truth of suffering, the truth of the origin of suffering, the truth of the cessation of suffering, and the truth of the path leading to this cessation. These Four Noble Truths are very explicitly and clearly exemplified in the life of ... the Buddha himself. I feel [it] is the same with the life of Christ. If you look at the life of Jesus, you will see all the essential practices and teachings of Christianity exemplified. And in the lives of both Jesus Christ and the Buddha, it is only through hardship, dedication and commitment, and by standing firm on one's principles that one can grow spiritually and attain liberation. That seems to be a central and common message.

*A*ny action, regardless of its significance, has an effect and leaves an imprint in the mind. And this action immediately affects the experience and the very world in which the individual is living. As far as that individual is concerned, the world has changed.
It is on this basis that Buddhists explain the inter-dependent nature of mind and matter, or mind and body. Of course, in Buddhism, the term karma would be used.

I feel there is tremendous convergence and a poten-tial for mutual enrichment through dialogue between the Buddhist and Christian traditions, especially in the area of ethics and spiritual practice, such as the practice of compassion, love, meditation and the en-hancement of tolerance. I feel that dialogue could go very far and reach a deep level of understanding.

To achieve a meaningful dialogue, a dialogue which would mutually enrich the two traditions, we need a foundation that is based on the clear recognition of the diversity that exists among humanity, the diverse mental dispositions, interests, and spiritual inclinations of the people of the world. For example, for some people, the Christian tradition, based on belief in a Creator, has a most powerful effect on their ethical life and serves to motivate them to act in an ethical and sound way. However, this might not be the case for every person. For others, the Buddhist tradition, which does not emphasise belief in a Creator, may be more effective. In the Buddhist tradition, there is an emphasis on a sense of personal responsibility rather than on a transcendent being.

It is also crucial to recognise that both spiritual traditions share the common goal of producing a human being who is a fully realised, spiritually mature, good and warm-hearted person. Once we have recognised these two points – commonality of the goal and the clear recognition of the diversity of human dispositions – then I feel there is a very strong foundation for dialogue.

*I*n Christianity there is an inspiring teaching about
turning the other cheek when struck by an enemy.
This same ideal underlies Buddhist philosophy.
Through a systematic practice, we can develop a
tolerance so powerful that when an enemy strikes
we feel actual appreciation for his actions, for the
opportunity for growth he has provided. We feel at
ease, free from anger and hate, and clearly see the
compulsions triggering his behaviour. We can feel
genuine compassion for the sad fate he brings upon
himself as a result of his harmful conduct.

ADDRESS TO YALE UNIVERSITY, USA,
OCTOBER 1991

*I*f one is always trying to look at things in terms of
similarities and parallels, there is a danger of rolling
everything up into one big entity ... I do not personally advocate seeking a universal religion. I don't think
it is advisable to do so.

*I*n general I am in favour of people continuing to follow the religion of their own culture and inheritance. Of course, individuals have every right to change if they find that a new religion is more effective or suitable for their spiritual needs. But, generally speaking, it is better to experience the value of one's own religious tradition. Here is an example of the sort of difficulty that may arise in changing one's religion. In one Tibetan family in the 1960s the father of the family passed away, and the mother later came to see me. She told me that as far as this life was concerned she was a Christian, but for the next life there was no alternative for her but Buddhism. How complicated! If you are a Buddhist, be a genuine Buddhist. Not something half-and-half. This will only cause confusion in your mind.

*F*orming a new world religion is difficult and not particularly desirable. However, in that love is essential to all religions, one could speak of the universal religion of love. As for the methods for developing love as well as for achieving salvation or permanent liberation, there are many differences between religions. Thus I do not think we could make one philosophy or one religion.

Furthermore I think that differences in faith are useful. There is a richness in the fact that there are so many different presentations of the way ... At the same time, the motivation of all religious practice is similar – love, sincerity, honesty. The way of life of practically all religious persons is contentment. The teachings of tolerance, love and compassion are the same. A basic goal is the benefit of humankind – each type of system seeking in its own unique way to improve human beings. If we put too much emphasis on our own philosophy, religion or theory, are too attached to it, and try to impose it on other people, it makes trouble. Basically all the great teachers, such as Gautama Buddha, Jesus Christ, or Mohammed, founded their new teachings with the motivation of helping their fellow humans. They did not mean to gain anything for themselves, nor to create more trouble or unrest in the world.

*R*eligion is like nourishment for your spirit and your mind. When embarking on a spiritual path, it is important that you engage in a practice that is most suited to your mental development, your dispositions and your spiritual inclinations. It is crucial that each individual seek a form of spiritual practice and belief that is most effective for that individual's specific needs. Through this, one can bring about an inner transformation, the inner tranquillity that will make that individual spiritually mature and a warm-hearted, whole, good and kind person. That is the consideration one must use in seeking spiritual nourishment.

*U*nity among religions is not an impossible idea. It is possible, and in the present state of the world it is especially important. Mutual respect would be helpful to all believers; and unity between them would also bring benefit to unbelievers. For the unanimous flood of light would show them the way out of their ignorance.

*I*n terms of human happiness, I feel it is not necessary to accept one particular religion. Without accepting a religion, but simply developing a realisation of the importance of compassion and love, and with that more concern and respect for others, a kind of spiritual development is very possible for those persons who are outside of religion.

ADDRESS AT WESTMINSTER ABBEY,
LONDON, 1985

*M*any people stress the necessity for faith and religion. Others say there is nothing beyond the senses. Buddhism, which is a spiritual path rather than a religion, is a bridge between the two.

IN CONVERSATION WITH THE EDITOR, 1989

*O*riginal Marxism was about how to distribute money, rather than how to make it, as in Capitalism. Buddhists could have gone along with that. Unfortunately, in practice, Communists used inhuman methods to gain and keep control.

IN CONVERSATION WITH THE EDITOR, 1989

I was always concerned with compassion even when I was a naughty little boy not at all interested in spirituality. When I saw human beings, poor people or animals, even insects, injured in some way, I always felt a strong compassion. In Lhasa, when I saw those poor sheep and yaks on their way to the slaughterhouse I felt an intolerable pain in the heart. I had to do something. I had some money, and I was able to buy them and save their lives. Of course I couldn't have gone on doing that indefinitely. Yet somehow I think that was one sign of the quality needed for being Dalai Lama. You know what I mean. Not an elevated being, just an ordinary human being with an active seed of compassion.

IN CONVERSATION WITH THE EDITOR, 1993

Wanted: A Spiritual Revolution

*Irrespective of different philosophies,
the most important thing is to
have a tamed and disciplined
mind and a warm heart.*

*I*t is my belief that if prayer, meditation and contemplation … are combined in daily practice, the effect on the practitioner's mind and heart will be all the greater. One of the major aims and purposes of religious practice for the individual is an inner transformation from an undisciplined, untamed, unfocused state of mind towards one that is disciplined, tamed and balanced … When meditation becomes an important part of your spiritual life, you are able to bring about this transformation in a more effective way.

*M*y call for a spiritual revolution is thus not a call for a religious revolution. Nor is it a reference to a way of life that is somehow other-worldly, still less to something magical or mysterious. Rather it is a call for a radical re-orientation away from our habitual preoccupation with self towards concern for the wider community of beings with whom we are connected, and for conduct which recognises others' interests alongside our own.

I believe there is an important distinction to be made between religion and spirituality. Religion I take to be concerned with belief in the claims to salvation of one faith tradition or another – an aspect of which is acceptance of some form of metaphysical or philosophical reality, including perhaps an idea of heaven or hell. Connected with this are religious teachings or dogma, ritual, prayers and so on. Spirituality I take to be concerned with those qualities of the human spirit – such as love and compassion, patience, tolerance, forgiveness, contentment, a sense of responsibility, a sense of harmony, which bring happiness to both self and others. Whilst ritual and prayer, along with questions of nirvana and salvation are directly connected with religious faith, these inner qualities need not be, however. There is thus no reason why the individual should not develop them, even to a high degree, without recourse to any religious or metaphysical belief system. This is why I sometimes say religion is something we can perhaps do without. What we cannot do without are these basic spiritual qualities.

*I*t is easier to meditate than actually do something for others. I feel that merely to meditate on compassion is to take the passive option. Our meditation should form the basis for action, for seizing the opportunity to do something.

*I*t is critical to serve others, to contribute actively to others' well-being. I often tell practitioners that they should adopt the following principle: regarding one's own personal needs, there should be as little involvement or obligation as possible. But regarding service to others, there should be as many involvements and obligations as possible. This should be the ideal of a spiritual person.

Consider our over-emphasis on material gain. There is a tendency to assume that this alone can provide us with all the satisfactions we require. Yet, by nature, the satisfactions it can provide will be limited to the level of the physical senses. If it were true that we human beings were no different from animals this would be fine. However, given the complexity of our species – in particular the fact that we experience thoughts and emotions as well as possess imaginative and critical faculties – it is obvious that our needs transcend the merely sensual. The prevalence of anxiety, stress, doubt, confusion, uncertainty and depression amongst those whose basic needs have been met is a clear indication of this. Our problems, both those we experience externally such as wars, crime and violence and those we experience internally as emotional and psychological suffering will not be solved until we address this underlying neglect of our inner dimension. That is why the great movements of the last hundred years and more – democracy, liberalism, socialism and Communism – have all failed to deliver the universal benefits they were supposed to provide, despite many wonderful ideas. A revolution is called for, certainly, but not a political, an economic or a technical revolution. We have had enough experience of these during the past century to know that a purely external approach will not suffice. What I propose is a spiritual revolution.

*W*hen Buddhists speak of Dharma, the Tibetan equivalent is *chii* which means 'transformation' or 'transforming power'. Compassion is, in many ways, the fundamental principle of the Dharma. However, compassion must be combined inseparably with wisdom. It is the union of wisdom and compassion that is the way, the Dharma.

*F*or a spiritual practitioner, one's enemies play a crucial role. As I see it, compassion is the essence of a spiritual life. And in order for you to become successful in practising love and compassion, the practice of patience and tolerance is indispensable. There is no fortitude similar to patience, just as there is no affliction worse than hatred.

ETHICS AND THE

GOOD SOCIETY

*It is in everybody's interest to seek those
[actions] that lead to happiness and
avoid those which lead to suffering.
And because our interests are inextricably
linked, we are compelled to accept ethics
as the indispensable interface between
my desire to be happy and yours.*

I see nothing wrong with material progress per se, provided *people* are always given precedence. In order to solve human problems in all their dimensions, we must combine and harmonise economic development with spiritual growth. However, we must know its limitations. Although materialistic knowledge in the form of science and technology has contributed enormously to human welfare, it is not capable of creating lasting happiness … Materialistic knowledge can only provide a type of happiness that is dependent upon physical conditions. It cannot provide happiness that springs from inner development.

*T*he most important use of knowledge and education is to help to understand the importance of engaging in more wholesome actions and bringing about discipline within our minds. The proper utilisation of our intelligence and knowledge is to effect changes from within to develop a good heart.

*E*ven though the training in ethics takes many forms, the ethics of abandoning the ten non-virtues is their basis. Of the ten non-virtues, three pertain to bodily actions, four to verbal actions and three to mental actions. The three physical non-virtues are:

1. Taking the life of a living being: ranging from killing an insect to killing a human.
2. Stealing: taking away another's property without his consent, regardless of its value, whether the deed is done by oneself or through another.
3. Sexual misconduct: committing adultery.

The four verbal non-virtues are:

4. Lying: deceiving others through spoken words or physical gestures.
5. Divisiveness: creating dissension by causing those in agreement to disagree or by causing those in disagreement to disagree still further.
6. Harshness: abusing others.
7. Senselessness: talking about foolish things motivated by desire and so forth.

The three mental non-virtues are:

8. Covetousness: thinking, 'May this become mine', desiring something that belongs to another.

9. Harmful intent: wishing to injure others, be it great or small injury.
10. Wrong view: viewing some existent thing, such as rebirth, cause and effect, or the Three Jewels,* as non-existent.

The opposites of these ten non-virtues are the ten virtues, and engaging in them is called the practice of ethics.

---

* The core of Buddhism: Buddha, his doctrine (Dharma), and the Spiritual Community.

Such human qualities as morality, compassion, decency, wisdom and so forth have been the foundations of all civilisations. These qualities must be cultivated and sustained through systematic moral education in a conducive social environment, so that a more humane world may emerge. The qualities required to create such a world must be inculcated right from the beginning, from childhood. We cannot wait for the next generation.

Compassion is what makes our lives meaningful. It is the source of all lasting happiness and joy. And it is the foundation of a good heart, the heart of one who acts out of a desire to help others. Through kindness, through affection, through honesty, through truth and justice toward all others, we ensure our own benefit ... There is no denying that if society suffers we ourselves suffer.

*I*t is not enough to make noisy calls to halt moral degeneration, we must do something about it. Since present-day governments do not shoulder such 'religious' responsibilities, humanitarian and religious leaders must strengthen the existing civic, social, cultural, educational and religious organisations to revive human and spiritual values. Where necessary we must create new organisations to achieve these goals. Only in so doing can we hope to create a more stable base for world peace.

*D*angerous consequences will follow when politicians and rulers forget moral principles. Whether we believe in God or karma, ethics is the foundation of every religion.

*E*stablishing binding ethical principles is possible when we take as our starting point the observation that we all desire happiness and not to suffer. We have no means of discriminating between right and wrong if we do not take into account others' feelings, others' sufferings. And if it is correct that this aspiration is a settled disposition shared by all, it follows that each individual has a right to pursue happiness and avoid suffering.

From this we can infer that one of the things which determines whether an act is ethical or not is its effect on another's – or others' – experience or expectation of happiness. An act which harms or does violence to this is potentially an unethical act.

*M*otivation is very important, and thus my simple religion is love, respect for others, honesty: teachings that cover not only religion but also the fields of politics, economics, business, science, law, medicine – everywhere. With proper motivation these can help humanity ... Without good motivation, science and technology, instead of helping, bring more fear and threaten global destruction. Compassionate thought is very important for humankind.

*W*hether you believe in God or not does not matter so much, whether you believe in Buddha or not does not matter so much. You must lead a good life. And a good life does not mean just good food, good clothes, good shelter. These are not sufficient. A good motivation is what is needed: compassion without dogmatism, without complicated philosophy; just understanding that others are human brothers and sisters and respecting their human rights and dignity. That we humans can help each other is one of our unique human capacities.

*I*t is not sufficient for religious people to be involved with prayer. Rather, they are morally obliged to contribute all they can to solving the world's problems.

I remember once an Indian politician taking me to task over this view. He said to me, quite humbly, 'Oh, but we are politicians, not religious people. Our first concern is with serving people through politics.' To which I replied, 'Politicians need religion even more than a hermit on retreat. If a hermit acts out of bad motivation, he harms no-one but himself. But if some-one who can directly influence the whole of society acts with bad motivation, then a great number of people will be adversely affected.'

$\mathcal{N}$ature's law dictates that, in order to survive, bees must work together. As a result, they instinctively possess a sense of social responsibility. They have no constitution, no law, no police, no religion or moral training, but because of their nature, they labour faithfully together. Occasionally, they may fight, but in general, based on co-operation, the whole colony survives. We human beings have a constitution, laws and a police force. We have religion, remarkable intelligence and a heart with a great capacity for love. We have many extraordinary qualities, but in actual practice, I think we are lagging behind those small insects. In some respects, I feel that we are poorer than the bees.

DEMOCRACY AND

HUMAN RIGHTS

*I believe in justice and truth,
without which there would be
no basis for human hope.*

STATEMENT ON THE FIFTH ANNIVERSARY
OF THE LHASA UPRISING,
10 MARCH 1974

I myself am convinced that government should always be by the will and through the co-operation of the people. I am ready to try to do whatever tasks my people ask of me, but I have no craving whatsoever for personal power or riches. I have no doubt at all that in this spirit and under the guidance of our religion, we shall mutually solve whatever problems confront us, and make a new Tibet, as happy in the modern world as old Tibet was in its isolation.

ON THE DRAWING UP OF A NEW
CONSTITUTION FOR A FUTURE TIBET

*N*o system of government is perfect, but democracy is closest to our essential human nature. As free individuals, we can use our unique intelligence to try to understand ourselves and our world. But if we are prevented from using our discrimination and creativity, we lose one of the basic characteristics of a human being.

CONFERENCE ON SECURITY AND CO-OPERATION
IN EUROPE, BUDAPEST, 1994

To my mind, democracy is more compassionate, more harmonious, more friendly than any other system. It respects others' rights and considers others equally as human brothers and sisters. Although you might dis-agree with them, you have to respect their wishes.

Although Communism espoused many noble ideals, it failed utterly because it relied on force to promote its beliefs. Brute force, no matter how strongly applied, can never subdue the basic human desire for freedom.

ADDRESS TO THE SECOND INTERNATIONAL CONFERENCE
OF NEW AND RESTORED DEMOCRACIES,
MANAGUA, NICARAGUA, JULY 1994

*W*hen democracy and human rights are under attack it is often the most gifted, dedicated and creative members of society who become the first targets … No system of government is perfect, but democracy is closest to our essential human nature; it is also the only stable foundation upon which a just and free global political structure can be built. So it is in all our interests that those of us who already enjoy democracy should actively support everybody's right to do so.

ADDRESS TO THE SECOND INTERNATIONAL CONFERENCE
OF NEW AND RESTORED DEMOCRACIES,
MANAGUA, NICARAGUA, JULY 1994

*A*s free human beings we can use our unique intelligence to try to understand ourselves and our world. But if we are prevented from using our creative potential, we are deprived of one of the basic characteristics of a human being.

ADDRESS TO NGOS AT THE UN WORLD
CONFERENCE ON HUMAN RIGHTS,
VIENNA, JUNE 1993

*G*eneral standards of human rights apply to the people of all countries because, regardless of their cultural background, all humans share an inherent yearning for freedom, equality and dignity. Democracy and respect for fundamental human rights are as important to Africans and Asians as they are to Europeans and Americans.

ARTICLE IN *HARVARD INTERNATIONAL REVIEW*,
1995

*B*rute force, no matter how strongly applied, can never subdue the basic human desire for freedom and dignity. It is not enough, as communist systems have assumed, merely to provide people with food, shelter and clothing. Human nature needs to breathe the precious air of liberty.

*W*hen we demand the rights and freedoms we so cherish, we should also be aware of our responsibilities. If we accept that others have an equal right to peace and happiness as ourselves, do we not have a responsibility to help those in need?

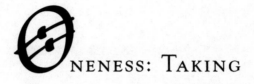

ONENESS: TAKING

RESPONSIBILITY FOR

THE WORLD

*The whole of humanity is
… one human family.
This planet is our only home.*

SPEECH TO THE OXFORD UNION SOCIETY,
DECEMBER 1991

Our planet is our house, and we must keep it in order and take care of it if we are genuinely concerned about happiness for ourselves, our children, our friends and other sentient beings who share this great house with us.

I believe that to meet the challenge of the next century, human beings will have to develop a greater sense of universal responsibility. Each of us must learn to work not just for his or her own self, family or nation, but for the benefit of all mankind.

SPEECH TO THE NEW YORK ALLIANCE
FOR WORLD SECURITY AND THE
COUNCIL OF FOREIGN RELATIONS,
NEW YORK, APRIL 1994

*B*ecause we all share this planet earth, we have to learn to live in harmony and peace with each other and with nature. That is not just a dream, but a necessity. We are dependent on each other in so many ways that we can no longer live in isolated communities and ignore what is happening outside those communities.

LECTURE AT OSLO UNIVERSITY,
DECEMBER 1989

*T*he universe we inhabit can be understood in terms of a living organism in which each cell works in balanced co-operation with every other cell to sustain the whole. If just one of these cells is harmed, as it is when disease strikes, that balance is harmed and there is danger to the whole. This in turn suggests that our individual well-being is intimately connected both with that of all others and with the environment within which we live. It also becomes apparent that our every action, our every deed, word and thought, no matter how slight or inconsequential it may seem, has an implication not only for ourselves but for all others too.

*T*oday we understand that the future of humanity very much depends on our planet, and that the future of the planet very much depends on humanity. This has not always been so clear to us. But now human use, population and technology have reached that certain stage where Mother Earth no longer accepts our presence with silence. In many ways she is now telling us, 'My children are behaving badly', she is warning us that there are limits to our actions.

*T*oday's world requires us to accept the oneness of humanity. In the past, isolated communities could afford to think of one another as fundamentally separate. Some could even exist in total isolation. But nowadays, whatever happens in one region eventually affects many other areas. Within the context of our inter-dependence, self-interest clearly lies in considering the interest of others.

ARTICLE BY HIS HOLINESS THE DALAI LAMA
IN *THE TIMES OF INDIA*, 11 APRIL 1993

*I*f we unbalance Nature, humankind will suffer. Furthermore, we must consider future generations: a clean environment is a human right like any other. It is therefore part of our responsibility towards others to ensure that the world we pass on is as healthy as, if not healthier than we found it. This is not quite such a difficult proposition as it might sound. For although there is a limit to what we as individuals can do, there is no limit to what a universal response might achieve. It is up to us as individuals to do what we can, however little that may be. Just because switching off the light on leaving the room seems inconsequential, it does not mean we shouldn't do it.

*R*esponsibility does not only lie with the leaders of our countries or with those who have been appointed or elected to do a particular job. It lies with each of us individually. Peace, for example, starts within each one of us.

LECTURE AT OSLO UNIVERSITY,
DECEMBER 1989

*O*n a certain day, month and year
One should observe the ceremony
Of tree-planting.
Thus, one fulfils one's responsibilities,
Serves one's fellow-beings
Which not only brings one happiness
But benefits all.

OCTOBER 1993

*I*t is necessary to help others, not only in our prayers, but in our daily lives. If we find we cannot help another, the least we can do is to desist from harming them. We must not cheat others or lie to them. We must be honest human beings ...

Simply as a member of the human family, we need this kind of attitude. It is through such an attitude that real and lasting world peace and harmony can be achieved.

*I*n this world, in order to enable society to develop, all its members have to assume responsibilities and make their contribution. If we do not make collective contributions then there will be no development.

SPEAKING TO THE TIBETAN NATIONAL ASSEMBLY
IN DHARAMSALA, MAY 1989

*B*elief in rebirth should engender a universal love,
for all living beings and creatures, in the course of
their numberless lives and our own, have been our
beloved parents, children, brothers, sisters, friends.
And the virtues our creed encourages are those which
arise from this universal love – tolerance, forbearance,
charity, kindness, compassion.

*W*hen the environment changes, the climatic
condition also changes. When the climate changes
dramatically, the economy and many other things
change. Our physical health will be greatly affected.
Conservation is not merely a question of morality,
but a question of our own survival.

Our world is becoming one community. We are being drawn together by the grave problems of over-population, dwindling natural resources, and an environmental crisis that threatens the very foundation of our existence on this planet. Human rights, environmental protection and greater social and economic equality are all interrelated. I believe that to meet the challenges of our times, human beings will have to develop a greater sense of universal responsibility. Each of us must learn to work not just for oneself, one's own family or nation, but for the benefit of all humankind. Universal responsibility is the key to human survival. It is the best foundation for world peace.

TIBET AND NON-VIOLENCE

I am a steadfast follower of the doctrine of non-violence which was first preached by Lord Buddha, whose divine wisdom is absolute and infallible and was practised in our own time by the Indian saint and leader, Mahatma Gandhi.

*W*hen Tibet was still free, we cultivated our natural
isolation, mistakenly thinking that we could prolong
our peace and security that way. Consequently, we paid
little attention to the changes taking place in the
world outside. Later, we learned the hard way that in
the international arena, as well as at home, freedom is
something to be shared and enjoyed in the company of
others, not kept to yourself.

BUDAPEST, 1994

*W*hen the Chinese Communist armies marched
into Tibet in 1950 ... it was many centuries since
Tibet had been a military power, for we believe in the
path of peace and have tried to follow it ever since the
wisdom of Lord Buddha was brought to our country
from India over a thousand years ago.

*F*or over a thousand years we Tibetans have adhered to spiritual and environmental values in order to maintain the delicate balance of life across the high plateau on which we live. Inspired by the Buddhist message of non-violence and compassion, and protected by our mountains, we sought to respect every form of life and to abandon war as an instrument of national policy.

ADDRESS TO THE EUROPEAN PARLIAMENT
IN STRASBOURG, JUNE 1988

*T*he attention of the world is riveted on Korea where aggression is being resisted by an international force. Similar happenings in remote Tibet are passing without notice. It is in the belief that aggression will not go unchecked and freedom unprotected in any part of the world that we have assumed the responsibility of reporting to the United Nations Organisation recent happenings in the border area of Tibet.

11 NOVEMBER 1950 – VAIN APPEAL BY THE
DALAI LAMA AND HIS TIBETAN GOVERNMENT
TO THE UNITED NATIONS, AFTER THE
CHINESE HAD INVADED TIBET

*W*e Tibetans have a unique and distinct cultural heritage just as the Chinese have. We do not hate the Chinese, we deeply respect the riches of Chinese culture which spans so many centuries. Though we have deep respect and are not anti-Chinese, we six million Tibetans have an equal right to maintain our own distinctive culture as long as we do not harm others. Materially we are backward, but in spiritual matters – in terms of the development of the mind – we are quite rich. We Tibetans are Buddhists, and the Buddhism which we practise is a rather complete form of Buddhism …

In the past century we remained a peaceful nation with our unique culture. Now unfortunately, during the last few decades this nation and culture are being deliberately destroyed. We like our own culture and our own land; we have the right to preserve it …

Also, materially backward or not, the six million Tibetans are human beings. We are six million human souls with the right to live as human beings. This is the problem.

*T*he sufferings which my people are undergoing are beyond description, and it is imperatively necessary that this wanton and ruthless murder ... should be brought immediately to an end. It is under these circumstances that I appeal to you and the United Nations in the confident hope that our appeal will receive the consideration it deserves.

LETTER FROM HIS HOLINESS THE DALAI LAMA TO DAG HAMMARSKJÖLD, THE SECRETARY-GENERAL OF THE UN, ON 9 SEPTEMBER 1959, A FEW MONTHS AFTER HIS ESCAPE TO INDIA

*T*ibet is far away, and other countries have their own fears and troubles. We can well understand that there may be a tendency to let the events in Tibet drift back into history. Yet Tibet is on this very earth. Tibetans are human; in their way they are very civilised; certainly they are sensitive to suffering. I would dare to say that no people have suffered more since the Second World War; and their sufferings have not ended, they are continuing every day, and they will continue until the Chinese leave our country, or until Tibetans have ceased to exist as a race or as a religious community.

*T*he question of the Tibetan national struggle is not just a political one, I believe it is a more spiritual involvement. I myself feel, as a Buddhist monk, that if the struggle were purely political, then I must consider whether my involvement is appropriate or not. But since this struggle is not only for political but also for spiritual freedom, which is of benefit not only to Tibetans but to other communities, I consider it as spiritual work and a part of my spiritual practice.

ADDRESS TO THE OXFORD UNION SOCIETY,
DECEMBER 1991

*O*urs has been a long struggle. We know our cause is just. Because violence can only breed more violence and suffering, our struggle must remain non-violent and free of hatred. We are trying to end the suffering of our people, not to inflict suffering upon others.

NOBEL PEACE PRIZE ACCEPTANCE SPEECH,
OSLO, DECEMBER 1989

*T*ibet – an ancient nation with a unique culture and civilisation – is disappearing fast. In endeavouring to protect my nation from this catastrophe, I have always sought to be guided by realism, moderation and patience. I have tried in every way I know to find some mutually acceptable solution in the spirit of reconciliation and compromise. However, it has now become clear that our efforts alone are not sufficient to bring the Chinese government to the negotiating table. This sad state of affairs compels me to appeal to your government and the international community for urgent intervention and action on behalf of my people ...

For our part, Tibetans will continue our non-violent struggle for freedom ... We will resist the use of violence as an expression of the desperation which many Tibetans feel. As long as I lead our freedom struggle, there will be no deviation from the path of non-violence.

'DEMOCRACY MUST FLOWER IN CHINA'
– STATEMENT TO A SPECIALLY CONVENED
HEARING ON TIBET BY THE FOREIGN AFFAIRS
COMMITTEE OF THE BUNDESTAG IN BONN,
JUNE 1995

*I*t is my dream that the entire Tibetan plateau should become a free refuge where humanity and nature can live in peace and in harmonious balance. It would be a place where people from all over the world could come to seek the true meaning of peace within themselves, away from the tensions and pressures of much of the rest of the world. Tibet could indeed become a creative centre for the promotion and development of peace.

LECTURE AT OSLO UNIVERSITY,
DECEMBER 1989

I have always envisioned the future of my own country Tibet, as a neutral, demilitarised sanctuary where weapons are forbidden and the people live in harmony with nature. I have called this a Zone of Ahimsa or non-violence. This is not merely a dream – it is precisely the way Tibetans used to live for over a thousand years before our country was tragically invaded.

SPEECH TO THE NEW YORK ALLIANCE
FOR WORLD SECURITY AND THE
COUNCIL ON FOREIGN RELATIONS,
NEW YORK, APRIL 1994

I believe that Truth will ultimately prevail. No
system can subdue Truth for ever.

IN CONVERSATION WITH THE EDITOR, 1989

*W*e Tibetans still have no feeling of hatred for the
great Chinese people, although their representatives in
Tibet have treated us so barbarously. Our only wish is
to live our own lives in peace and friendship with all
our neighbours, including the Chinese.

*T*he Chinese are human beings like ourselves. They
are our eastern neighbours. Nothing is going to change
that, so it would be better for us to live in friendship
with them, sharing each other's troubles.

IN CONVERSATION WITH THE EDITOR, 1989

I am working not for Tibet's separation from China but towards a solution where Tibet's separate and distinct identity can co-exist and develop within the framework of an open and tolerant China.

STATEMENT ON THE ELEVENTH ANNIVERSARY OF THE
TIANANMEN SQUARE REVOLT, JUNE 2000

I believe that Tibet will be free only when its people become strong, and hatred is not strength. It is a weakness. The Lord Buddha was not being religious, in the popular sense of the term, when he said that hatred does not cease by hatred. Rather, he was being practical. Any achievement attained through hatred [can only invite] trouble sooner or later.

STATEMENT, 10 MARCH 1971

*T*he Tibetan people have a deep trust, believing that the Dalai Lama will bring them freedom. But I am only a Buddhist monk. I have only the strength of compassion and the strength that my cause is a just cause.

ADDRESS, 1996

*N*on-violence means dialogue, using our language, the human language. Dialogue means compromise; respecting each other's rights; in the spirit of reconciliation there is a real solution to conflict and disagreement. There is no hundred percent winner, no hundred percent loser – not that way but half-and-half. That is the practical way, the only way.

*V*iolence ultimately leads to the betrayal of even the noblest cause.

SPEAKING TO A YOUTH CONFERENCE
ON NON-VIOLENCE,
BELFAST, OCTOBER 2000

*Y*ou see, a nation is dying. My strength comes from the justice of my cause, and I think from my compassion. But I need help. Not just a few nice words, but some kind of action.

ADDRESS, 1996

I accept that the Chinese have committed atrocities, but though I feel sad and angry I don't go to the extent of wanting them to suffer. That kind of attitude is forbidden by Buddhism. We do curse and rant, but real hatred never arises. I feel that whatever wrong the Chinese may have done, it's not their fault. If I ever allowed myself to think that certain people were undeserving of happiness, then I should have broken my Bodhisattva vow.

IN CONVERSATION WITH THE EDITOR, 1993

FORGIVING THE ENEMY

*In my own experience, the period of
greatest gain in knowledge and experience
is the most difficult period in one's life ...
Through a difficult period, you can learn, you
can develop inner strength, determination,
and courage to face the problem. Who
gives you this chance? Your enemy.*

Since China invaded Tibet in 1949–1951, we have struggled to keep our cause alive and preserve our Buddhist culture of non-violence and compassion. It would be easy to become angry ... to feel nothing but hatred for the Chinese authorities. Labelling them as the enemy, we could self-righteously condemn them for their brutality and dismiss them as unworthy of further thought or consideration. But that is not the Buddhist way ...

Our most valuable teachers are our enemies. Not only is this a fundamental Buddhist teaching, it is a demonstrated fact of life. While our friends can help us in many ways, only our enemies can provide us with the challenge we need to develop tolerance, patience and compassion ... three virtues essential for building character, developing peace of mind, and bringing us true happiness.

ADDRESS AT YALE UNIVERSITY, USA,
OCTOBER 1991

*I*f you can cultivate the right attitude, your enemies are your best spiritual teachers because their presence provides you with the opportunity to enhance and develop tolerance, patience and understanding. By developing greater tolerance and patience, it will be easier for you to develop your capacity for compassion, and through that, altruism. So even for the practice of your own spiritual path, the presence of an enemy is crucial.

*N*ow, there are many, many people in the world, but relatively few with whom we interact, and even fewer who cause us problems. So, when you come across such a chance for practising patience and tolerance, you should treat it with gratitude. It is rare. Just as having unexpectedly found a treasure in your own house, you should be happy and grateful to your enemy for providing that precious opportunity.

*T*he realisation that another person wishes to harm and hurt you cannot undermine genuine compassion – a compassion based on the clear recognition of that person as someone who is suffering, someone who has the natural and instinctual desire to seek happiness and overcome suffering, just like oneself.

*W*hen other beings, especially those who hold a grudge against you, abuse and harm you out of envy, you should not abandon them, but hold them as objects of your greatest compassion and take care of them.

*I*n spite of the atrocious crimes which the Chinese have committed in our country, I have absolutely no hatred in my heart for the Chinese people … We should not seek revenge on those who have committed crimes against us, or reply to their crimes with other crimes. We should reflect that by the law of karma, they are in danger of lowly and miserable lives to come, and that our duty to them, as to every being, is to help them to rise towards Nirvana, rather than let them sink to lower levels of rebirth.

*W*e should not lose our compassion whatever the circumstances. One Tibetan monk, whom I knew very well in Namgyal Monastery in the Potala in Lhasa, explained this important task. He spent more than seventeen years in Chinese labour camps and during those years he said that on a few occasions he faced danger. I asked him what kind of danger: I thought it must be a danger to his life. But he answered, danger of losing compassion towards the Chinese. I couldn't practise that, I think, but under such difficult circumstances, he actually practised it.

INTERVIEW WITH MIRI HEATHERWICK IN
RESURGENCE, MAY/JUNE 2000

SUFFERING,

IMPERMANENCE AND DEATH

*Within the framework of the Buddhist Path,
reflecting on suffering has tremendous
importance because by realising the nature of
suffering, you will develop greater resolve to
put an end to the causes of suffering and the
unwholesome deeds which lead to suffering.
And it will increase your enthusiasm for
engaging in the wholesome actions and deeds
which lead to happiness and joy.*

*P*eople in particular, unlike other living beings, create disturbances for themselves and others by reason of differences such as of country, race, political system and theory. As a result of these differences, groups of men are amassed, war is made and so on. [As if] intentionally putting a finger in its own eye, mankind consciously engages in techniques that bring various undesirable consequences upon itself: causes for fear, man-made diseases, starvation and untimely death.

*W*e should quickly seize enlightenment while we still have the chance. In much less than a century all of us will be dead. We cannot be sure that we will be alive even tomorrow. There is no time to procrastinate. I who am giving this teaching have no guarantee that I will live out this day.

*I*t is extremely important to investigate the causes or origins of suffering. One must begin that process by appreciating the impermanent, transient nature of our existence. All things, events and phenomena are dynamic, changing every moment, nothing remains static. Meditating on one's blood circulation could serve to reinforce this idea: the blood is constantly flowing, it never stands still ... And since it is the nature of all phenomena to change every moment, this indicates to us that all things lack the ability to endure or remain the same. And since all things are subject to change, nothing exists in a permanent condition, nothing is able to remain the same under its own independent power. Thus, all things are under the power or influence of other factors. So at any given moment, no matter how pleasant or pleasurable your experience may be, it will not last.

*F*or me personally, the strongest, most effective practice to help tolerate suffering is to see and understand that suffering is the underlying nature of Samsara, of unenlightened existence.

*A*s a Buddhist monk, my concern extends to all members of the human family and, indeed, to all sentient beings who suffer. I believe all suffering is caused by ignorance. People inflict pain on others in the selfish pursuit of their own happiness or satisfaction. Yet true happiness comes from a sense of brotherhood and sisterhood. We need to cultivate a universal responsibility for one another and the planet we share.

NOBEL PEACE PRIZE ACCEPTANCE SPEECH,
OSLO, DECEMBER 1989

*T*here is an Indian saying: if you are struck by a poisonous arrow, it is important first to pull it out, there is no time to ask who shot it, what sort of poison it is and so on. First handle the immediate problem, and later we can investigate. Similarly, when we encounter human suffering, it is important to respond with compassion rather than question the politics of those we help. Instead of asking whether their country is enemy or friend, we must think, 'These are human beings, they are suffering, and they have a right to happiness equal to our own.'

*O*ur attitude towards suffering is very important because it can affect how we cope with it when it arises. Our usual attitude consists of an intense aversion and intolerance of our own pain and suffering. However, if we can transform our attitude, adopt an attitude that allows us greater tolerance of it, this can do much to help counteract feelings of mental unhappiness, dissatisfaction and discontent.

*W*e also often add to our pain and suffering by being overly sensitive, over-reacting to minor things, and sometimes taking things too personally.

I think that there is one aspect to our experience of suffering that is of vital importance. When you are aware of your pain and suffering, it helps you to develop your capacity for empathy, the capacity which allows you to relate to other people's feelings and sufferings. This enhances your capacity for compassion towards others.

*F*eelings of grief and anxiety are a natural human response to a loss. But if feelings are left unchecked, they can lead to a kind of self-absorption. A situation where the focus becomes your own self. You become overwhelmed by the sense of loss, and you get a feeling that it's only you who's going through this. Depression sets in. But in reality, there are others who will be going through the same kind of experience … It may help to think of the other people who have similar or even worse tragedies. Once you realise that, then you no longer feel isolated, as if you have been single-pointedly picked out. That can offer you some kind of consolation.

*I*t is our suffering that is the most basic element that we share with others, the factor that unifies us with all living creatures.

One important aspect of my daily practice is its concern with the idea of death. To my mind, there are two things that, in life, you can do about death. You can choose to ignore it, in which case you may have some success in making the idea of it go away for a limited period of time. Or you can confront the prospect of your own death and try to analyse it and, in so doing, try to minimise some of the inevitable sufferings it causes. Neither way can you actually over-come it. However, as a Buddhist, I view death as a normal process of life … Knowing that I cannot escape it, I see no point in worrying about it.

$\mathcal{Y}$ou might consider things like old age and death as negative, unwanted, and simply try to forget about them. But eventually those things will come anyway. If you've avoided thinking about them, they will come as a shock causing an unbearable mental unease. However, if you spend some time thinking about old age, death and so on, your mind will be much more stable when these things happen ... That's why I believe it can be useful to prepare yourself ahead of time by familiarising yourself with the kinds of suffering you might encounter ... But you should not forget the fact that this does not alleviate the situation. It may help one mentally to cope, but it does not alleviate the problem itself.

WORLD PEACE

Wars arise from a failure to understand one another's humanness. Instead of summit meetings, why not have families meet for a picnic and get to know each other while the children play together?

ADDRESS, 1981

*T*he necessary foundation for world peace and the ultimate goal of any new international order is the elimination of violence at every level. For this reason the practice of non-violence surely suits us all. It simply requires determination, for by its very nature non-violent action requires patience. While the practice of non-violence is still something of an experiment on this planet, if it is successful it will open the way to a far more peaceful world in the next century.

*I*nternal peace is an essential first step to achieving peace in the world, true and lasting peace. How do you cultivate it? It's very simple. In the first place by realising clearly that all mankind is one, that human beings in every country are members of one and the same family.

ADDRESS, 1985

*E*verybody loves to talk about calm and peace whether in a family, national, or international context. But without inner peace how can we make real peace? World peace through hatred and force is impossible. Even in the case of individuals, there is no possibility to feel happiness through anger. If in a difficult situation one becomes disturbed internally, overwhelmed by mental discomfort, then external things will not help at all. However, if despite external difficulties or problems, internally one's attitude is of love, warmth, and kind-heartedness, then problems can be faced and accepted.

*D*eep in my mind I see that borders are not so fundamental. People consider borders very important, even a few inches of their sacred land. I feel it doesn't matter. We should have maximum interaction across the borders. Peace is more important. People should have a happy life, a happy community. So I believe the Tibetans and Chinese really can live happily together.

INTERVIEW WITH MIRI HEATHERWICK
IN *RESURGENCE*, MAY/JUNE 2000

On receiving the Nobel Peace Prize, October 1989

When I first heard the rumour I was in California. It was evening. I was a little bit excited. Then I listened to a BBC news bulletin. No mention there. I thought 'Oh well', and went to bed. Next morning I got up at the usual time at 4 and was told it had been announced on the radio. But by then the excitement was already gone.

IN CONVERSATION WITH THE EDITOR, 1990

War brings only suffering … Even if we are victorious, that victory means sacrificing many people. It means *their* suffering. Therefore the important thing is peace.

*R*eal peace [is] not just the absence of violence or of war ... A mere absence of war is not genuine, lasting world peace. Peace must develop on mutual trust. And since weapons are the greatest obstacle [to the] development of mutual trust, I think the time has now come to figure out how to get rid of these weapons ... We must make our ultimate goal very clear: the whole world should be demilitarised.

*T*he next century should be a century of dialogue and discussion rather than one of war and bloodshed.

MESSAGE FOR THE NEW MILLENNIUM,
JANUARY 2000

For fear of offending China, the Dalai Lama was not invited to the UN Millennium World Peace Summit of Spiritual Leaders held in New York in August 2000! He sent a message to the meeting, however. When his New York representative read this out to the assembly, Chinese religious leaders walked out in protest. Below are two extracts.

It is my belief that whereas the twentieth century has been a century of war and untold suffering, the twenty-first century should be one of peace and dialogue. As the continued advances in information technology make our world a truly global village, I believe there will come a time when war and armed conflict will be considered an outdated and obsolete method of settling differences among nations and communities. The nations and peoples of the world will soon realise that dialogue and compromise are the best methods of settling differences for mutual benefit and for the sake of our future and that of our much ravaged and fragile planet ...

*T*here can be no peace as long as there is grinding poverty, social injustice, inequality, oppression, environmental degradation and as long as the weak and small continue to be down-trodden by the mighty and powerful.

*P*eace, in the sense of absence of war, is of little value to someone who is dying of hunger or cold. It will not remove the pain of torture inflicted on a prisoner of conscience. It does not comfort those who have lost their loved ones in floods caused by senseless deforestation in a neighbouring country. Peace can only last where human rights are respected, where the people are fed, and where individuals and nations are free. True peace with oneself and with the world around us can only be achieved through the development of mental peace.

LECTURE AT OSLO UNIVERSITY,
DECEMBER 1989

INVITATION TO ACTION

I pray for all of us, oppressor and friend, that together we may succeed in building a better world through human understanding and love, and that in doing so we may reduce the pain and suffering of all sentient beings. Thank you.

NOBEL PEACE PRIZE ACCEPTANCE SPEECH,
OSLO, DECEMBER 1989

*N*ever give up
No matter what is going on
Never give up.
Develop the heart.
Too much energy in your country is spent
Developing the mind instead of the heart.
Be compassionate not just to your friends
     but to everyone
Be compassionate.
Work for peace in your heart and in the world.
Work for peace and I say again
Never give up.
No matter what is happening,
No matter what is going on around you,
Never give up.

QUOTED IN THE JOURNAL OF THE
TIBET SOCIETY OF THE UNITED KINGDOM,
WINTER 1999/2000

Some people are really showing excitement about the new millennium, that the new millennium itself will bring happy days. I think that is wrong. Unless there is a new millennium inside, then the new millennium itself will not change much – same days and nights, same sun and moon. The important thing is transformation, new ways of thinking.

MESSAGE FOR THE NEW MILLENNIUM,
JANUARY 2000

May the force of observing that which is right
And abstinence from wrong practices and evil deeds
Nourish and augment the prosperity of the world.
May it invigorate living beings and help them blossom.
May sylvan joy and pristine happiness
Ever increase, ever spread and encompass all that is.

PART OF A POEM WRITTEN TO MARK THE OPENING OF
THE INTERNATIONAL CONFERENCE ON ECOLOGICAL
RESPONSIBILITY: A DIALOGUE WITH BUDDHISM,
NEW DELHI, OCTOBER 1993

With my two hands joined, I appeal to you, the reader, to ensure that you make the rest of your life as meaningful as possible. Do this by engaging in spiritual practice if you can. As I hope I have made clear, there is nothing mysterious in this. It consists in nothing more than acting out of concern for others. And provided you undertake this practice sincerely and with persistence, little by little, step by step, you will gradually be able to re-order your habits and attitudes so that you think less about your own narrow concerns and more of others. In doing so, you will find that you enjoy peace and happiness yourself.

Relinquish your envy, let go your desire to triumph over others. Instead try to benefit them. With kindness, with courage and confident that in doing so you are sure to meet with success, welcome others with a smile. Be straightforward. And try to be impartial. Treat everyone as if they were a close friend. I say this neither as Dalai Lama nor as someone who has special powers or ability. Of these I have none. I speak as a human being, one who like yourself wishes to be happy and not to suffer. If you cannot for whatever reason be of help to others, at least don't harm them.

I should like to share with you a prayer composed by Shanti Deva, an eleventh-century Indian Buddhist master, in the hope that it will provide for you the same inspiration and determination as it continues to give to me:

> For as long as space endures
> And for as long as sentient beings remain
> Until then may I, too, abide
> To dispel the misery of the world.

POSTSCRIPT

Tenzin Gyatso, the Fourteenth Dalai Lama, was born in north-eastern Tibet on 6 July 1935 and discovered as the new Dalai Lama just over two years later. Brought to Lhasa (central Tibet), aged only four years, he was installed amid great pomp and ceremony in 1939. Eleven years later, when Mao Tse-tung's Communists had come to power in mainland China, and his People's Liberation Army had already marched into and occupied Tibet's eastern regions, Tenzin Gyatso was hurriedly enthroned in Lhasa as Head of State, three years ahead of his majority. With Tibet facing the greatest danger it had ever known, a fifteen-year-old boy was now its secular as well as its spiritual leader.

The story of what followed has been told many times and there is no space for it here. The Chinese Communists' occupation of central Tibet, their attempt to strip the Dalai Lama and his Cabinet of all status and power, the eruption of eastern Tibet

in revolt, and finally, when the Tibetans suspected
that their beloved leader was about to be abducted to
China, the Lhasa Uprising of 1959, the escape of the
Dalai Lama to India and the beginning of all-out
martial law inside central as well as eastern Tibet.
(See, among others, my own books, *Tears of Blood*,
HarperCollins 1993 and *Kundun*, HarperCollins
1997.) There followed years of isolation, merciless
indoctrination, terror, starvation, revenge killings,
arbitrary imprisonment in gulags and reform-through-
labour camps, culminating in the horrors of the
Cultural Revolution, that vicious onslaught on everything old which, in Tibet, lasted from 1966 till after
the death of Mao ten years later. After that there
was some slight improvement, as reforms were put
in place and visitors began to be admitted. But after
the mid 1980s when the Chinese authorities began
settling large numbers of their own people in Tibet,
the situation deteriorated rapidly. Revolts in 1987,
1988 and 1989 were bloodily put down by tanks, riot
squads and armoured cars – but at least those atrocities were witnessed by journalists and other visitors
from the West, who proceeded to tell the outside
world about them. It was now that, in growing numbers, people in the West began to take stock of what
had been done to Tibet.

It is now over fifty years since the Chinese occupied Tibet and claimed it as an inseparable part of the Motherland. Few Tibetans have ever consented to their domination, though they have had to pay lip-service to it in order to stay alive and out of prison. Over the years, this fact – that, in spite of decades of repression and brainwashing, Tibetans have never lost their sense of separateness and have continued to cling to their own, basically religious culture – has been borne in on the Chinese. As a result, since 1995, the situation has become worse rather than better, as a frenetic crusade against Buddhism has been launched, an all-out attempt to eradicate, once and for all, every trace of Tibetan-ness from Tibet. This crusade against the Buddhist religion, the Tibetan language and the Dalai Lama himself is so virulent that it has been called a new Cultural Revolution. Monks and nuns have been ordered not only to renounce their alle-giance to the Dalai Lama – they must sign a formal document doing so – but to condemn and vilify him. Those who refuse are expelled from their monasteries, dragged off to prison, or both. In some cases, when the non-acceptance has been universal, the monasteries have been destroyed. Those that remain are now completely under Communist control. Nor are lay people immune from this persecution. House-to-house

searches, usually at the dead of night, for pictures
of or cassettes by the Dalai Lama are commonplace.
Government workers and officials have been ordered
to remove their children from monasteries and nun-
neries in the capital, and all have been warned that
if they participate in religious activities their children
will be expelled from school. Teachers have been
ordered to extol the merits of atheism, and a hotline
has been set up for those who are prepared to denounce
any Tibetans who continue to practise their religion.

The spiritual heart is thus being ripped out of Tibet,
and no one can begin to imagine where the present
terror will end. It is against this hate-filled background
that the exiled Dalai Lama travels the world with his
message of peace, love, forgiveness and, above all,
hope.

$\mathcal{S}$ OURCES

In addition to the specific sources cited, the following publications have been drawn upon. Unless stated otherwise, these books have been written by His Holiness the Dalai Lama.

Ancient Wisdom, Modern World: Ethics for a New Millennium, Little, Brown & Co., USA, 1989.

The Art of Happiness: A Handbook for Living, His Holiness the Dalai Lama and Howard Cutler, Hodder & Stoughton, 1998.

The Buddhism of Tibet and *The Key to the Middle Way*, Harper & Row, USA, 1975.

Cultivating a Daily Meditation, Library of Tibetan Works and Archives, 1991.

The Dalai Lama at Harvard: Lectures on the Buddhist Path to Peace, Snow Lion, USA, 1984.

The Dalai Lama's Book of Daily Meditations: The Path to Tranquillity, Rider, 1998.

The Dalai Lama's Book of Wisdom: Insights on Daily Living, Compassion and Justice, ed. Matthew E. Bunson, Rider, 1997.

Freedom in Exile, Hodder & Stoughton, 1990.

The Good Heart: The Dalai Lama Explores the Heart of Christianity and of Humanity, Rider, 1996.

His Holiness the Dalai Lama: the Bodhgaya Interviews, Snow Lion, USA, 1988.

Kindness, Clarity and Insight, Snow Lion, USA, 1984.

My Land and My People, Potala, USA, 1983.

My Tibet, His Holiness the Dalai Lama with Galen Rowell, University of California Press, 1991.

The Spirit of Tibet: Universal Heritage – Selected Speeches and Writings of His Holiness the Dalai Lama XIV, ed. A. A. Shiromany, Allied Publishers Ltd, India, 1995.